GENESIS 1-11

THEOLOGY OF WORK PROJECT

GENESIS
1-11

THE BIBLE AND YOUR WORK
Study Series

HENDRICKSON
PUBLISHERS

Theology of Work
The Bible and Your Work Study Series: Genesis 1–11

© 2014 by Hendrickson Publishers Marketing, LLC
P.O. Box 3473
Peabody, Massachusetts 01961-3473

ISBN 978-1-61970-514-2

Adapted from the *Theology of Work Bible Commentary*, copyright © 2014 by the Theology of Work Project, Inc. All rights reserved.

William Messenger, Executive Editor, Theology of Work Project
Sean McDonough, Biblical Editor, Theology of Work Project
Patricia Anders, Editorial Director, Hendrickson Publishers

Contributors:
Christopher Gilbert, "Genesis 1–11" Bible Study
Andrew Schmutzer and Alice Mathews, "Genesis 1–11" in the *Theology of Work Bible Commentary*

The Theology of Work Project is an independent, international organization dedicated to researching, writing, and distributing materials with a biblical perspective on work. The Project's primary mission is to produce resources covering every book of the Bible plus major topics in today's workplaces. Wherever possible, the Project collaborates with other faith-and-work organizations, churches, universities and seminaries to help equip people for meaningful, productive work of every kind.

Printed in the United States of America

First Printing – November 2014

Contents

The Theology of Work

Work is not only a human calling but also a divine one. "In the beginning God created the heavens and the earth." God worked to create us and created us to work. "The LORD God took the man and put him in the garden of Eden to till it and keep it" (Gen. 2:15). God also created work to be good, even if it's hard to see in a fallen world. To this day, God calls us to work to support ourselves and to serve others (Eph. 4:28).

Work can accomplish many of God's purposes for our lives—the basic necessities of food and shelter, as well as a sense of fulfillment and joy. Our work can create ways to help people thrive. Our work can discover the depths of God's creation. Our work can bring us into wonderful relationships with co-workers and those who benefit from our work (customers, clients, patients, and so forth).

Yet many people face drudgery, boredom, or exploitation at work. We have bad bosses, hostile relationships, and unfriendly work environments. Our work seems useless, unappreciated, faulty, frustrating. We don't get paid enough. We get stuck in dead-end jobs or laid off or fired. We fail. Our skills become obsolete. It's a struggle just to make ends meet. But how can this be if God created work to be good—and what can we do about it? God's answers to these questions must be somewhere in the Bible, but where?

The Theology of Work Project's mission has been to study what the Bible says about work and to develop resources to apply the Christian faith to our work. It turns out that every book of the Bible gives practical, relevant guidance that can help us do our jobs better, improve our relationships at work, support ourselves, serve others more effectively, and find meaning and value in our work. The Bible shows us how to live all of life—including work—in Christ. Only in Jesus can our work be transformed to become the blessing it was always meant to be.

To put it another way, if we are not following Christ during the 100,000 hours of our lives that we spend at work, are we really following Christ? Our lives are more than just one day a week at church. The fact is that God cares about our life *every day of the week*. But how do we become equipped to follow Jesus at work? In the same ways we become equipped for every aspect of life in Christ—listening to sermons, modeling our lives on others' examples, praying for God's guidance, and most of all by studying the Bible and putting it into practice.

This Theology of Work series contains a variety of books to help you apply the Scriptures and Christian faith to your work. This Bible study is one volume in the series The Bible and Your Work. It is intended for those who want to explore what the Bible says about work and how to apply it to their work in positive, practical ways. Although it can be used for individual study, Bible study is especially effective with a group of people committed to practicing what they read in Scripture. In this way, we gain from one another's perspectives and are encouraged to actually *do* what we read in Scripture. Because of the direct focus on work, The Bible and Your Work studies are especially suited for Bible studies *at* work or *with* other people in similar occupations. The following lessons are designed for thirty-minute lunch breaks, although they can be used in other formats as well.

Christians today recognize God's calling to us in and through our work—for ourselves and for those whom we serve. May God use this book to help you follow Christ in every sphere of life and work.

Will Messenger, Executive Editor
Theology of Work Project

Introduction

Genesis 1–11

Whether you're writing an essay, cleaning a house, or designing a bridge, to do it well requires some sense of plan and purpose. It takes thoughtfulness in advance to work from a promising beginning to a satisfying end.

Genesis is the biblical book where work begins. It provides us the vision and mission for every form of human work, in other words, the deep "why?" and "what?" of work. All other biblical books draw from its understanding. This one book provides a window into God's work, the work of creating our world. Here we discover that he locates us in geographical places, where time passes, with material resources, and sources of energy—all the stuff underlying our own labors today. Genesis engages the real world we know, not some disembodied spiritual plane, and it is in this world that God relates especially to humankind—people made in his image. We can say that Genesis shows us from the very beginning how God designed us to work *in* his world, *on* his world, *with* his world, and *for* his world.

Seeing God at work in Genesis, we learn how he intends for us to participate in work that he designed. And we discover that the Creator of all uses our obedience, and even our disobedience, to

further that work. While every book of the Bible will contribute
something to our understanding of work, Genesis proves to be
the fountain from which the Bible's theology of work flows. Here
are some of the themes we will explore in this study:

Genesis 1–3

- God's creation and the kind of participation he planned
  for us

- The boundaries he set for us in which to work

- The freedom to work in loving relationship or not

- The consequence on our work of the first human family
  choosing "or not"

Genesis 4–11

- The more urgent necessity of work because humanity is
  fallen and the world is not the way it was meant to be

- The sovereign justice and mercy of God in working to
  redeem the world and setting new boundaries and opportunities for us in participating with him

- What a mercy work is and what amazing opportunity
  we are given to assist in the redemption of the world in
  which we find ourselves

- The contrast of Noah working in harmony with God ver-
  sus the city of Babel that wanted power and achievement
  on its own terms

Before you undertake this study, think about your current attitude to this creation account of God. What are you hoping you

might learn about your work from this study as outlined above? Pause for a few moments of silence to reflect and then offer a prayer in your own words or as follows:

Lord,

As I undertake this study, please open my heart to new things, things I don't know. Instead of leaning on my own understanding, help me to hear your word.

Amen.

Chapter 1

God Creates the World

(Genesis 1:1–2:3)

Lesson #1: God at Work in Making the Universe (1:1–25)

Joyful Engagement in Messy Creation

A bricklayer's overalls get spattered with mortar and hands toughen in the laying of bricks. A chef's apron protects from blood and juices in the preparation of meat and vegetables. Just as we might enjoy physical engagement in our work, so in Genesis we see God immersed with the elements of the world he is making. Formless matter delights him as he develops it into a harmony of things, living and inanimate, which are good in his sight. At the height of his creative work he seems to get down and dirty: "The Lord God formed man from the dust of the ground" (Gen. 2:7).

 Food for Thought

What does it look like for God to be immersed in his creation today? How have you seen God get "down and dirty"?

_____

_____

_____

_____

_____

_____

_____

_____

God is at work while creating. Even though it is with astonishing power—by a spoken word—yet a power that orders everything step by step to build toward the next thing, and the next thing, so that at completion all things harmonize. This display of God's infinite power, beautifully ordered in the text, reassures us that he will never run out of gas but can and will redeem the brokenness we know too well. His use of power by a spoken word does *not* mean that God's creation is not work, any more than writing a computer program or acting in a play is not work. In Genesis 2 and 3, we see him sculpt the human form, plant a garden, tend an orchard, and tailor skins for clothing.

Finally, we should note that there is no sharp distinction between the material and the spiritual in Genesis. The *ruah* of God in Genesis 1:2 is "breath," "wind," and "spirit." "The heavens and the earth" (Gen. 1:2 and 2:1) are not two separate realms but a Hebrew merism meaning "the universe" in the same way that the English merism "kith and kin" means "relatives." The rest of the Bible confirms Genesis's perspective about this, for the Bible ends where it begins—on earth. Humanity does not depart the earth to join God in heaven. Instead, God perfects his kingdom on earth and calls into being "the holy city, the new Jerusalem, coming down out of heaven from God" (Rev. 21:2).

Food for Thought

How do you regard the material world? As beautiful and worthy of effort? Or a sinking ship to escape from to an immaterial "heaven"? How does this Genesis view of the physical world change the meaning of your work?

_____

_____

_____

_____

_____

_____

_____

_____

Prayer

Pause for a few moments of silence to reflect on what you've just studied. Then offer a prayer, either spontaneous or by using the following:

> Lord,
>
> *I am amazed at the way you enjoy your work and are so engaged in the infinite details of the making of our world. Grant me to discover order and joy in the outworking of my own tasks.*
>
> *Amen.*

Lesson #2: God Is the Source of Creation (1:11) and He Works Relationally (1:26a)

An Identity Apart from Work

God creates everything, but he also literally sows the seed for the perpetuation of creation through the ages (1:11). The creation is forever dependent on God, "In him we live and move and have our being" (Acts 17:28), yet it remains distinct. And so, we are not animated like programmed robots to participate in his creation. Our work has the beauty and value of its arising from distinct beings who deserve a byline, just as a reporter is acknowledged as contributor to the daily newspaper. The stuff of our work indeed has its source in God, yet our completed products have their own weight and dignity.

 Food for Thought

How might our perspective on work differ if we were "programmed robots"? If we are "reporters" deserving a byline, what responsibilities do we have to God?

_____

_____

_____

_____

_____

Work from Loving Relationship

Even before God creates people, he speaks in the plural, "Let *us* make humankind in our image" (Gen. 1:26). It's difficult to be sure exactly what the ancient Israelites would have understood the plural to mean here, but it does demonstrate God working relationally. From the ministry of Jesus, especially in John's Gospel, we understand that "Let *us*" refers to the Trinity of Father, Son, and Holy Spirit. God is indeed in relationship with himself—and with his creation—in a Trinity of love. From John 1:14—Jesus, "the Word made flesh"—is present and active in creation from the beginning.

> In the beginning was the Word, and the Word was with God and the Word was God. He was in the beginning with God. All things came into being through him, and without him not one thing came into being. What has come into being in him was life, and the life was the light of all people. (John 1:1–4)

As Christians, we acknowledge our Trinitarian God—Father, Son, and Holy Spirit—is personally active in creation.

 Food for Thought

What implications are there for our relationship to our products in seeing God as distinct from his products? How do you see your work in relation to yourself? And since we understand God as a pre-existing community of three persons active in the work of creation, what can we learn from that for our own work life experience?

_____

_____

_____

_____

_____

Prayer

Pause for a few moments of silence to reflect on what you've just studied. Then offer a prayer, either spontaneous or by using the following:

Lord,

Help me to live in the freedom of an identity that is distinct from the products I make or the services I deliver. And, help me to seek unity of purpose with those I work alongside, in the making of things or serving of others.

Amen.

Lesson #3: God Limits His Work (2:1–3)

> God saw everything that he had made, and indeed, it was very good. And there was evening and there was morning, the sixth day. Thus the heavens and the earth were finished, and all their multitude. And on the seventh day God finished the work that he had done, and he rested on the seventh day from all the work that he had done. (Gen. 1:31–2:2)

Completion and Rest

Here we see that after six days of God's creative power, chaos has become an inhabitable environment, an extraordinary eco-system supporting every living thing God has made. The establishment of the world is complete. This doesn't mean that God ceases working, for as Jesus said, "My father is still working" (John 5:17). And as we shall see, God leaves plenty of work for us to do to develop the world he's given us to live in.

But at his completion, God crowns his six days of work with a day of rest. While creating humanity is the climax of God's creative work, resting on the seventh day is the climax of God's creative week. So why does God rest? There is majesty in God creating the universe and our habitable earth by speaking it into being. It's a clear implication from chapter 1 that God is not at all tired by the effort. He doesn't *need* to rest. Yet he chooses to limit his creation in the sequence of time as well as in space.

 Food for Thought

How is the work God is currently doing the same or different from his work at Creation? How does rest help us in our busy lives?

_____

_____

_____

_____

_____

The universe is a finite space, despite its largeness. It also has a beginning in time, attested by Genesis, and now scientific observers are in agreement as they find more and more evidence for a "big bang" origin. Neither the Bible nor science provide clear testimony of our universe having an endpoint in time, but God gives time a limit *within* the world as we know it. As long as time is running, God blesses six days for work and one for rest. There is more to God's life than work. And so we discover there is a limit to work that God himself observes, and it later becomes his command to people (Exod. 20:8–11).

 *Food for Thought*

Our text doesn't tell us why God rested after completing his work of establishing a habitable universe. But from your own experience what does life beyond work look like? How does it assist you to limit work to make space for that? What is the experience of work when it is not put under time limits?

_____

_____

_____

_____

_____

_____

_____

_____

Prayer

Pause for a few moments of silence to reflect on what you've just studied. Then offer a prayer, either spontaneous or by using the following:

Lord,

Thank you for showing us that it's your character to rest from work and make space for rest—reflection, recreation, and to receive the thanks and praise of those for whom you have made all things. Help me value the rest as much as the work and so reflect this part of your nature.

Amen.

Chapter 2

God Creates and Equips People to Work—Part 1

(Genesis 1:26–2:25)

Lesson #1: People are Created in God's Image (1:26–27; 5:1)

> God said, "Let us make humankind in our image, according to our likeness. God created humankind in his image, in the image of God he created them; male and female he created them."
>
> (Gen. 1:26–27)

> When God created humankind, he made them in the likeness of God. (Gen. 5:1)

The Meaning of Personhood

All creation displays God's design, power, and goodness, but only human beings are said to be made in God's image. In this chapter, our concern is to understand what being made in the likeness of God means for our work. Obviously, we can't create universes and we aren't found outside of time, like God. Yet for all the constraints of being creatures in particular places on earth and at particular times in history, we find in ourselves the ability to work in a material world, in relationship, and observe limits to work, even as God does with his creation.

 *Food for Thought*

How do our particular constraints—such as the times and places in which we live—influence our perspectives on our work?

_____

_____

_____

_____

_____

_____

Five ways in which we have been made like God are described in the remainder of chapter 1 and through chapter 2: (1) dominion, (2) relationships, (3) fruitful growth, (4) provision, and (5) limits. There are two accounts of this, in Genesis 1:26–2:4 and 2:4–25. The first explains what it means to work in God's image, and the second shows how God equips Adam and Eve for their work as they begin life in the Garden of Eden. Each account deals with the same five likenesses of God.

We discover that we are given the mandate (the authority) to act, and with the capacity to do so comes the responsibility to act. For the remainder of this chapter and through the next, we will look at each of these God-likenesses from the perspective of how to work like God and with what equipment we have been given for this work.

But we should remain mindful that we can't create worlds out of nothing. And we shouldn't try to do everything God does. For example, "Beloved, never avenge yourselves, but leave room for the wrath of God; for it is written, 'Vengeance is mine, I will repay, says the Lord'" (Rom. 12:19).

 *Food for Thought*

What do you think of when you hear the words *likeness* or *image of*? How does that affect your understanding of this Genesis account of our created capabilities? And what does it suggest about our value to God and our place in his creation?

_____

_____

_____

_____

_____

_____

_____

_____

Prayer

Pause for a few moments of silence to reflect on what you've just studied. Then offer a prayer, either spontaneous or by using the following:

Lord,

> *It is astonishing to look at ourselves in a mirror and realize that you have given us capabilities in this world that are like yours, however constrained they are by our locations and our historical moment. Please help us rise to the responsibilities we have, here and now, as children of God, to make our world a better place.*

> *Amen.*

Lesson #2: Made for Dominion (1:26; 2:5)

The Exercise of Dominion

> "Have dominion over the fish of the sea, and over the birds of the
> air, and over the cattle, and over all the wild animals of the earth,
> and over every creeping thing that creeps upon the earth."
>
> (Gen. 1:26)

When God gives mankind this dominion over the earth, we recognize the implication. It's a delegated authority with real accountability. While it's our fundamental role to be kings over the earth, like regents under an emperor, we have the dignity of responsibility for our patch of the world—to take care of its growth and development for the sake of the generations to follow.

 Food for Thought

What have you done to care for your patch of the world for generations to follow? How would you like the world to look for future generations?

_____

_____

_____

_____

_____

In this way we mirror God, who is the source of our image-bearing, so that our work and way of working is based on his original work and serves his wise purposes.

Equipped for Dominion

> No plant of the field was yet in the earth and no herb of the field
> had yet sprung up—for the LORD God had not caused it to rain
> upon the earth, and there was no one to till the ground.
>
>   (Gen. 2:5)

In this account, creation could not be completed until God
provided people to develop it to its fullest extent. Theologian
Meredith Kline explains, "God's making the world was like a
king's planting a farm or park or orchard, into which God put
humanity to 'serve' the ground and to 'serve' and 'look after'
the estate."

When we hear the word *dominion*, it can carry the ring of *tyranny*, and *subdue* might also be heard as *subjugate*. But these
are not the meanings in Genesis. Dominion is the power to work
for God's creation, not the authority to work *against* it. Dominion over all living creatures is a contract from God to care for
them, and so properly exercised, *dominion* takes responsibility
for the welfare of the places we are given to care for. In subdu-
ing the earth, we protect the resources we have—we don't just
exploit them. Remembering that the air, water, land, plants,
and animals are good (Gen. 1:4–31) reminds us that we are
meant to sustain and preserve the environment. Our work can
either preserve or destroy the clean air, water, and land, the
biodiversity, the ecosystems and biomes with which God has
blessed his creation. And it also means that we will govern our
self-interested behaviors so as to leave a better world for our
children's children.

Food for Thought

Consider the work you do. As an image-bearer of God, how might your work better reflect the Creator? How would this affect the choice of products or services you deliver? How would it affect the type of people you serve? And as someone meant to tend the garden (Gen. 2:15), for the sake of others too, how in your own occupation might you better care for the people and the environment entrusted to you?

_____

_____

_____

_____

_____

_____

_____

Prayer

Pause for a few moments of silence to reflect on what you've just studied. Then offer a prayer, either spontaneous or by using the following:

Lord,

It's a humbling realization that you entrust us with dominion over the earth. Please assist us to think more deeply and be more strategic in the care of our communities and our planet through the work we are given to do.

Amen.

Lesson #3: Made for Relationship (1:27; 2:18, 21–25)

Designed for Work with Others

As images of a relational God, we are inherently relational. The second part of Genesis 1:27 makes the point again, for it speaks of us not individually but in twos: "Male and female he created them." Relationships are a fact in Genesis, not a philosophical abstraction. God talks and works with Adam in naming the animals (Gen. 2:19), and God visits Adam and Eve "in the garden at the time of the evening breeze" (Gen. 3:8).

Scripture goes to the very core of God's *being* as Love—a love flowing back and forth among the Father, the Son (John 17:24), and the Holy Spirit. This love also flows out of God's being to us, doing nothing that is not in our best interest, and this has implications for the way we work with our colleagues. We are called to love the people we work with, among, and for. It is a moral responsibility.

 Food for Thought

How do we show love practically in the workplace?

_____

_____

_____

_____

_____

_____

Equipped to Work with Others

> "It is not good that the man should be alone; I will make him a helper as his partner." (Gen. 2:18)

For the first time, something is *not good*—the image of God remains incomplete in the solitary man. So God makes a woman out of the flesh and bone of Adam himself. When Eve arrives, Adam is filled with joy: "This at last is bone of my bones and flesh of my flesh" (Gen. 2:23). The union of the pair is so close, it is said that "they become one flesh" (Gen. 1:25). Although it *is* a romantic union, it is also a working relationship. Eve is created as Adam's *helper* and *partner* who will join him in working the Garden of Eden. To be a helper means to work. To be a partner means to work *with* someone.

The word translated as *helper* here (Hebrew *ezer*) is a word used elsewhere in the Old Testament to refer to God himself. "God is my helper [*ezer*]" (Ps. 54:4). "Lord, be my helper [*ezer*]" (Ps. 30:10). So an *ezer* is not a subordinate. Eve is not only a *helper* but also a *partner*. That's the same as our word, *co-worker*. Certainly, this is the sense of Genesis 1:27, "male and female he created them," which makes no distinction of priority or dominance. Domination of women by men—or vice versa—perverts God's good creation.

In Genesis 2:19, we see God delegate the naming of the animals to Adam, and the transfer of God's authority is genuine. "Whatever the man called every living creature, that was its name" (Gen. 2:19). God gave up the power of naming the animals so that Adam's power of naming would be real. In turn, when we delegate authority to other people, we give up some measure of our power and independence and take the risk of letting others' work affect us.

 *Food for Thought*

How does our perspective on work change if we think of ourselves as helpers? How does God's delegating authority influence the ideas of personhood and work?

_____

_____

_____

_____

_____

_____

_____

Finally, many people form some of their closest relationships when work provides a common purpose and goal. This makes possible the vast, complex array of goods and services beyond the capacity of any individual to produce—cars, computers, courier services, legislatures, mission agencies, schools, and so forth. The intimate relationship between a man and a woman results in families and makes possible a growing community to help tend the garden and make the whole earth fruitful. So our work and our community are thoroughly intertwined gifts from God. Together they provide the means for us to be fruitful and multiply.

 *Food for Thought*

If love is at the heart of the work of each person of the Trinity, consider how love might impact the way you think about your relationships with colleagues at work. What was the most meaningful, satisfying work project you have been part of? Can you identify the elements that made for that experience? How do they relate to this teaching from Genesis?

_____

_____

_____

_____

_____

_____

_____

Prayer

Pause for a few moments of silence to reflect on what you've just studied. Then offer a prayer, either spontaneous or by using the following:

Lord,

It seems to be our greatest challenge in this life to love others as you have loved us. Please give us courage in our work and our homes to foster trust and relational honesty. Make us able to help and be helped, co-labor, and share responsibility.

Amen.

Chapter 3

God Creates and Equips People to Work—Part 2

(Genesis 1:26–2:25)

Lesson #1: Made for Fruitfulness and Growth (1:28; 2:15, 19–20)

The Likeness of God Visible in Products of Beauty

If you have ever wandered through a weekend market, you have seen the volume of crafts produced by the vendors and often the extraordinary beauty of these items—crafts in metals, timbers, fabrics, various stones, and even carved gourds. Or perhaps you're more fascinated by bridges and buildings, visual art, theater, music, or automobiles and aircraft.

These products of our humanity arise from what theologians call the "creation mandate" or "cultural mandate" to be fruitful and multiply and to fill the earth. How remarkable that God entrusts us with developing the world he gave us! It *is* our work that prepares food and drink, writes stories, crafts products and services, rears children, educates students, and designs the institutions that serve our communities. The most excellent of these have a beauty that reflects back praise and glory to their source—the Creator.

Where does beauty fit in? God's work is not only productive but also a *delight to the eyes* (Gen. 3:6). Sometimes Christians seem to forget the value of beauty in God's eyes, and churches don't always make room for the arts—except, of course, for music with words about Jesus! We might all do better at valuing the beauty found in every field of human work, while remaining aware of its inherent danger, the allure of worshipping our creations rather than the Creator.

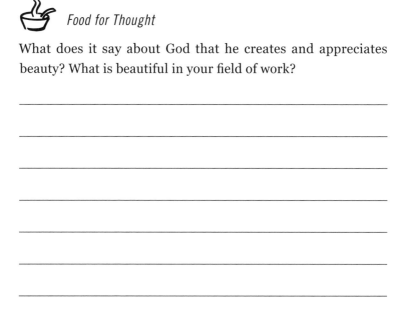 *Food for Thought*

What does it say about God that he creates and appreciates beauty? What is beautiful in your field of work?

_____

_____

_____

_____

_____

_____

_____

Equipped to Bear Fruit and Multiply

"The LORD God took the man and put him in the garden of Eden to till it and keep it" (Gen. 2:15). These two words in Hebrew, *avad* ("work" or "till") and *shamar* ("keep"), are also used for worship of God and keeping his commandments, respectively. A task done according to God's design has an unmistakable holiness, whether done at church or in the workplace.

The tasks given to Adam and Eve relate to discovering and physically developing the earth's resources. By naming what we discover in the process of our various tasks, we gain a deeper understanding of the part of God's creation that we're developing—science and theology working hand in hand (Gen. 2:19–20). This work is as diverse as every person God made, and limited only by his imagination and the limits he sets. Even a cursory look at the animal or plant worlds—in our travels, picture books, documentaries, and our own neighborhoods—suggests that his imagination is infinite. For ourselves, every task requires our imagination to guide us where to begin and where we expect to arrive. Likewise, developing God's creation into human products requires imagination. Every product was first an idea in the mind. Every job came from someone's imagining of a product or service and developing a process to make it actual.

 Food for Thought

Where do you experience a sense of fruitfulness in human effort? Do you experience it in beauty? How does that guide you in regard to your own work? How do you experience work as worship? How does your work/worship utilize your imagination?

_____

_____

_____

_____

_____

_____

_____

Prayer

Pause for a few moments of silence to reflect on what you've just studied. Then offer a prayer, either spontaneous or by using the following:

Lord,

It pleases you as worship when we offer fruitful and beautiful products from the earth's resources, for the benefit of our communities. Give us a deeper share of your wonderful imagination to delight you more with our work.

Amen.

Lesson #2: God's Provision (1:29–30; 2:8–14) and Limits (2:3; 2:17)

God Provides for Us

Everything we depend on for life comes ultimately from God. If we ever need to be reminded of this, all it takes is a little time in the garden trying to grow our own food. God's daily provision of air, water, earth, sunshine, and the miraculous growth of living things is what nourishes everyone on the planet. Facing our dependence on God's providence is the great leveler of hubris regarding our achievements. Despite our technologies, we have no power to tame the weather or choose the circumstance of our birth, nor can we avoid death. But acknowledging his power can give us that confident humility to ask and look for his involvement in our lives, including the work we do. In Matthew 6:28–33, Jesus assures us that God is deeply committed to providing what we need.

Food for Thought

Describe "confident humility."

_____

_____

_____

_____

_____

_____

_____

How God Provides for Us

> The Lord God planted a garden in Eden, in the east; and there he
> put the man whom he had formed. (Gen. 2:8)

God provides and we work with his provision. He plants and we
till. So the second cycle of the creation account shows us something of *how* God provides for our needs. In the arts, as well as
the sciences, we discover ever more resources that he designed
into the world as we apply ourselves to our creation mandate.
In addition to food, he created the earth with everything necessary for the flourishing of life on our planet. Spend a moment
listing the resources of the earth, the sea, and the sky, even the
accumulated knowledge of human intelligence at work, that are
benefiting our lives today.

Food for Thought

What would flourishing look like in your work environment?

_____

_____

_____

_____

_____

_____

_____

_____

Blessed By the Limits God Sets

> God blessed the seventh day and hallowed it, because on it God
> rested from all the work that he had done in creation. (Gen. 2:3)

The fourth of the Ten Commandments tells us that God's rest
is meant as an example for us to follow (Exod. 20:8–11). If the
Triune God makes it clear that there is more to life than work—
from which he rests—we who bear his image can only gain from
the limit he sets for himself and for us.

Jesus said clearly that God made the Sabbath for our benefit
(Mark 2:27). What are we to learn from this? When we cease
from work one day out of seven, we acknowledge that our life
is not defined only by work or productivity. Theologian Walter
Brueggemann put it this way, "Sabbath provides a visible testimony that God is at the center of life—that human production
and consumption take place in a world ordered, blessed, and

restrained by the God of all creation." As we humbly rely on God as provider, in Sabbath rest from our labors, we also renounce our sense of autonomy.

Food for Thought

What would be the dangers of autonomy?

_____

_____

_____

_____

_____

_____

_____

God Equips People to Work within Limits

> "You may freely eat of every tree in the garden; but of the tree of the knowledge of good and evil you shall not eat, for in the day that you eat of it, you shall die." (Gen. 2:16–17)

In the midst of the Garden of Eden, God plants two trees—the tree of life and the tree of the knowledge of good and evil (Gen. 2:9). Here God gives Adam and Eve specific instructions limiting their work: don't make use of the tree of the knowledge of good and evil.

Theologians have speculated at length about why God would put a tree in the Garden of Eden that he didn't want the inhabitants to use. Whatever the answer may be, it applies also to the world around us today. There are options available to us that are not good to make use of. If we want to work *with* God, rather than *against* him, we must choose to observe the limits he sets, rather than chasing after everything we might imagine is possible in creation. Could Adam and Eve love and trust God sufficiently to surrender their own desires and obey his command about the tree? God expects that those in relationship with him will respect the limits that bring about his good outcomes in his world.

 Food for Thought

Consider the industry you are a part of. In what ways does it depend on the resources God provides, and how are those resources utilized to benefit others? What ethical limits govern your field of work, and what are the benefits of maintaining them? What are the consequences when those limits are ignored?

_____

_____

_____

_____

_____

_____

_____

_____

Prayer

Pause for a few moments of silence to reflect on what you've just studied. Then offer a prayer, either spontaneous or by using the following:

Lord,

How humbling it is to see the riches of resource invested in our world for us to bless others. Thank you that almost every field of human enterprise acknowledges you by the limitations laid out in unique ethical considerations. This too is from you. Help us to know and promote those limits with gladness, in order to gain the highest good for the greatest number of people.

Amen.

Lesson #3: The Work of the "Creation Mandate"— A Summary (1:28; 2:15)

Our Need to Work

We often think of work as something we'd rather not do but are stuck with—"working for the weekend" and "Thank God it's Friday." But actually, a drive to work is built into us at the deepest level. If we are prevented from working for a long time—say, by illness, disability, or unemployment—it feels as though we are losing a part of ourselves. "There is no greater agony than bearing an untold story inside you," said writer Maya Angelou. Work undone is a story untold. As we have seen in Genesis, we are designed to contribute to the growth and flourishing of the earth and its people in our own moment of history—whether that means maintaining clean toilets, marketing toothbrushes, or designing a vehicle.

Decisions that affect people's ability to work are weighty matters, not just economically but also emotionally, socially, and spiritually. The decision to hire, fire, or lay off employees affects far more than their income. It judges their value and worth. It shapes their sense of self. Workers are part of an economic equation—the value of the products and services we produce must be more than the cost of the raw materials and our labor—but we are not *only* economic factors. Pope John Paul II said, "The value of human work is not primarily the kind of work being done but the fact that the one who is doing it is a person." As workers, we must be treated as people not as human "resources." Every decision affecting employment needs to be made with respect, fairness, humility, care, and love.

 Food for Thought

How does your work contribute to others' flourishing? What are the social, emotional, and spiritual matters that influence your work? How can we avoid treating others as "resources"?

_____

_____

_____

_____

_____

_____

_____

Likewise political and economic policies that affect employment are deeply spiritual, and not merely technical. Taxes, subsidies, and budget surpluses or deficits may create or destroy opportunities and incentives to work. Licenses, regulations, and zoning laws may accomplish a civic purpose at the cost of job opportunities. Good schools develop their students' God-given ability to work, while poor schools snuff out a lifetime of opportunities.

The decisions we make that affect our own ability to work are also deeply spiritual. When we apply for a job, or decide not to, show up on time ready to work, or come late and unprepared, we are making an assessment about our own ability and worth. When we work hard and creatively, or when we simply go through the motions, we show not only what we think of our employer but also of ourselves.

Finally, the way we treat people on the margins of the workforce says a lot about in whom we see the image of God. Imagine if our organization were skilled at creating true opportunities for people often overlooked for employment—for example, immigrants still learning English, people with intellectual or physical disabilities, or those facing racial, gender, or age discrimination.

Considering these types of issues, we see just small facets of the "Creation Mandate" or "Cultural Mandate" given to our first parents, by God our maker.

> God blessed them, and God said to them, "Be fruitful and multiply, and fill the earth and subdue it; and have dominion over the fish of the sea and over the birds of the air and over every living thing that moves upon the earth." (Gen. 1:28)

> The Lord God took the man and put him in the garden of Eden to till it and keep it. (Gen. 2:15)

Food for Thought

Consider the elements of the cultural mandate we have explored. How does your workplace value the people it employs, and how do you regard your employer? What change of attitude in employer or employees might assist your workplace to become more involved with a big picture of human flourishing? What could you do to assist that process?

_____

_____

_____

_____

_____

_____

_____

Prayer

Pause for a few moments of silence to reflect on what you've just studied. Then offer a prayer, either spontaneous or by using the following:

Lord,

You have dignified our race with an opportunity to partner with you in the development of an entire planet, which can be lived out in any task in any location at any time. Help us to hold onto this reality, whatever the circumstances of our employment, and be ambassadors for your creation mandate, wherever we are found.

Amen.

Chapter 4

People Fall into Sin in Work

(Genesis 3)

Lesson #1: The Lie that Divides (3:1–5)

Yes, But . . .

By now we should be feeling a sense of, "Yes, but . . ." The first two chapters of Genesis describe the world as it was originally meant to be. But we know it is decidedly *not* like that now. Work can be drudgery. We have bad bosses, dead-end jobs, office politics, grinding toil, crop failures, unemployment, wages too low to live on, and strife with co-workers. And so we come to Genesis 3, the story of the Fall. This gives us God's perspective on something we know from our work—that things have gone wrong in the world of work.

Take, for example, office politics. When people scheme to advance their own project or career, they may try to manipulate you for their own benefit. The first step is to isolate you and gain your confidence in order to make it easier to prey on your vulnerabilities. "I shouldn't really be telling you this, so keep it to yourself, but if this plan goes through, it could really hurt the career of everyone who didn't come from her department—like you." The next step is to sow fear, uncertainty, and doubt by distorting the truth. "Did she say she would give you a role in the implementation? Sure she will—you'll get to do the paperwork while she takes the credit." The next step is to offer a solution that appears to offer you control over the situation, but in reality puts you under the schemer's thumb. "I'll tell the boss you've found some problems with her plan. Put the things I've told you into our report, and you'll be the hero." The last step to recruit you is to exploit your relationships to help advance the plot. "You're friends with Hernando and Ellen—see if you get them on board too."

When someone wants to subvert a plan favored by their colleagues for their own plan, they will recast the narrative that defines the project. It's a triangulation, setting up a three-way dramatic moment of decision. There are the two people with their project narratives, and a team that needs to decide between the two. When one narrative gives reason to doubt the other, the doubt will probably take root in a team's perception. Then, confidence in the original leader erodes until his/her plan becomes impossible for the team to implement. The team then seeks the alternative. It's a risky strategy because it can destroy the unity of a team. And if the team is evenly divided, it can wreck the possibility of either proposal being implemented. A strategy of triangulation is evil when it distorts the narrative it is challenging, or lies about its details and seeks to divide a group as a means to aggrandize the new author, rather than a common good. A challenge that misrepresents a plan or a person is often called a strategy of "divide and conquer," or "splitting."

 *Food for Thought*

How does the idea of relationality contrast with the idea of negative office politics? How can we promote community instead of subversion?

_____

_____

_____

_____

We see this pattern of deception and manipulation played out in Genesis 3:1–6. A malevolent adversary of God, in the form of a serpent, targets an apparent vulnerability in Eve. He separates her from Adam and maneuvers her into what looks like a sincere chat about her experience of God. He distorts the truth by emphasizing the limits imposed by God, instead of the wide world of opportunity and abundance God gives. He suggests that real meaning and purpose can be found by acquiring her own source of wisdom instead of relying on God's. Doubt about God takes root in Eve. The serpent offers a solution—eat the fruit of the tree of the knowledge of good and evil, and find out for yourself what God is up to. Eve buys into the serpent's distorted view and eats the fruit. Then she offers it to her husband and he does the same.

This vain attempt to become "like God" in some way *beyond* what they already were as God's image-bearers (Gen. 3:5) backfires. Instead of becoming more like God, they become more distant from him. Instead of walking with God in the cool of the day as they used to do, they hide themselves from God. The only wisdom they gain is a knowledge of evil, the sophistication to prefer their own practical, aesthetic, and sensual tastes over God's truth. The control over their own destiny offered by the serpent turns out to be nothing but the self-destruction of their community of freedom and prosperity.

 Food for Thought

Consider positive and negative examples of "divide and conquer," "splitting," or "triangulating" that you have experienced in work or school environments. How did you navigate the dilemma it set? Do you know when you are most vulnerable to doubt about others, including God? What strategies might you employ to help resolve moments like these when your loyalty is tested?

_____

_____

_____

_____

_____

Prayer

Pause for a few moments of silence to reflect on what you've just studied. Then offer a prayer, either spontaneous or by using the following:

Lord,

I know that I am vulnerable to my own desires for self-advancement in work, play, and family life. Please walk with me and help me in the moments of doubt, temptation, and internal conflict to hear clearly from your word and wise counselors, by your Spirit, to know what is best. Please keep me from the evil one.

Amen.

Lesson #2: The Wreck of Relationships (3:6–13)

The broken relationships that we see among Adam, Eve, and God are mirrored in the broken relationships we face at work today. How quickly do relationships between bosses and workers break down? How prevalent is sexual harassment and rape within our institutions? How easily do leaders punish workers for problems caused by their own laziness? How frequently do colleagues scapegoat a fellow for a team error? Or climb over their peers by taking credit for someone else's achievement? Most of us experience such events in work and life, and they impinge on our ability to form honorable and productive relationships.

Food for Thought

Think about the questions posed above and discuss.

_____

_____

_____

_____

_____

_____

The Blame Game

When Adam and Eve chose to step out of bounds from God, they fractured all the relationships built into their very beings. When once they might walk and talk with their Creator in the cool of the evening breeze, now they hide from him as if he were the harsh and dangerous tyrant of the Serpent's narrative (Gen. 3:8).

Adam is estranged from Eve, blaming her for his decision to eat the fruit and blaming God for giving him the woman! "The woman whom you gave to be with me, she gave me fruit from the tree, and I ate" (Gen. 3:12). What fear, what confusion, what avoidance is this! She is no longer "flesh of my flesh and bone of my bone" in delightful unity of care for the garden. She is now *the woman,* with an ominous foreboding of the denigration, subjugation, and violence that will befall women at the hands of men in the ages to come.

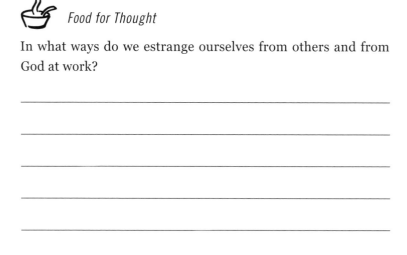 *Food for Thought*

In what ways do we estrange ourselves from others and from God at work?

_____

_____

_____

_____

_____

Eve's response also illustrates how fear and confusion have entered into human experience. She pushes the blame down the line to the serpent she entertained: "Then the LORD God said to the woman, 'What is this that you have done?' The woman said, 'The serpent deceived me, and I ate'" (Gen. 3:13). Perhaps this is akin to saying that the "devil made me do it," rather than admitting a deeper issue: an inordinate desire that made her vulnerable to accept a distortion of God's character so as to ignore his prohibition. So the man and the woman both justify their own behavior at the expense of breaking the ties that made them one flesh. How much less might the damage had been if they had said to God, "If you blame him (or her), blame me too, for we did it together"?

And so, estranged from God and estranged from each other, they're also estranged from the creatures given to them to care for. They're now untrustworthy to care for the garden, as we shall see more fully in exploring the consequences spelled out by God for their foolishness.

 Food for Thought

When breaches in relationships occur, it is often hard to see our own responsibility in the heat of the moment. Time passing can bring better perspective, although the damage is done. Where in your work life have you or others experienced such estrangement? In what way did casting blame play into that experience? Was there an experience of apology and reconciliation? How hard is it to move on past such events?

_____

_____

_____

_____

_____

_____

_____

Prayer

Pause for a few moments of silence to reflect on what you've just studied. Then offer a prayer, either spontaneous or by using the following:

> *Lord,*
>
> *We know that in every relational failure, the temptation is to run from responsibility and project blame onto others, or even on you, by citing circumstances beyond our control. Please help us to turn from fear and confusion towards trust in your steadfast love, so we might face our own part in the brokenness of our life at work and home. Help us be your agents of the new creation.*
>
> *Amen.*

Lesson #3: God Names the Consequences (3:14–24)

Merciful Judgment

Now comes God speaking judgment against this original sin by declaring consequences for the three participants—the serpent (Gen. 1:14), Eve (Gen. 3:16), and Adam (Gen. 3:17–18). The outcome for the man and the woman is hardship and toil affecting all human relationships, including work. The woman will face great pain in delivering children and also experience conflict through her desire for the man. The man must toil to wrest a living from the ground, which will produce "thorns and thistles" alongside the desired crop. Human beings will still do the work they were created to do, and God will still provide for their needs (Gen. 3:17–19). But work becomes more difficult and frustrating, with the strong possibility of failure.

Food for Thought

Which attributes does God display in his judgment of creation?

_____

_____

_____

_____

_____

_____

_____

_____

When Work Became Toil against Twin Evils

It is important to note that when work became toil, it was not the beginning of work. Work began in the garden as we have seen, a blessing flowing from the man and woman's likeness to God. After the Fall, work became more important—not less—because now more work is required to cope with the brokenness of the created order.

Where once the pair lived in freedom and pleasure, now they live under threat from the very elements from which they were derived—the man from the soil returning to the soil (Gen. 3:19), and the woman from the side of the man now dominated by the man before she too returns to the soil (Gen. 3:16). Death and domination seem normal now to the sin-sick human race, alien to God's plan and purpose.

 *Food for Thought*

What things—such as death and domination—seem normal to us but are not part of God's original creation?

_____

_____

_____

_____

_____

_____

_____

And so we live today toiling against twin evils. One is a perilous earth of fire, flood, drought, earthquake, tsunami, parasites, disease, and so much more. The other is human immorality—hurting those we are made to love, excluding them from the benefits of our work, exploiting natural resources for the inordinate profit of an elite few with little care for the workers, the resident people, plants, and animals, and all the while, perverting the knowledge of God's character in order to deny accountability. In the next chapter we will explore the outworking of these consequences.

Food for Thought

How would you illustrate the difference between "toil" and "work" in your own experience? What are the frustrations you experience in your field of work and how do you deal with them? Which of them is "broken-earth" evil, and which comes from human immorality? How does this brokenness affect your sense of God's character?

_____

_____

_____

_____

_____

_____

Prayer

Pause for a few moments of silence to reflect on what you've just studied. Then offer a prayer, either spontaneous or by using the following:

> *Lord,*
>
> *So much that we turn our hands to is affected by the randomness of a disordered natural world, and this is intensified by the human propensity for violence and personal aggrandizement. It seems so overwhelming when we read about the haphazard results of the toiling of the nations every day in the news. Grant that we might find ourselves accepting the toil in our work in the way that you did, when you lived among us.*
>
> *Amen.*

Chapter 5

People Work in a Fallen Creation

(Genesis 4–8)

When God drives Adam and Eve from the Garden of Eden (Gen. 3:23–24), they take with them their fractured relationships and toilsome work. God, however, continues to provide for them (Gen. 3:21), and the curse does not destroy their ability to multiply (Gen. 4:1–2) or to attain a measure of prosperity (Gen. 4:3–4). Work is now a mixture of creation and repair, success and failure, joy and sorrow. There is much more to do now than there was in the garden. Work is not less important to God's plan but more.

Lesson #1: The First Murder (4:1–25)

The Violence of the Line of Cain

In this next scene of human origins, two brothers—a shepherd and a farmer—receive a different response from God when they offer him the fruit of their work. Abel is commended for providing his very best lamb (Gen. 4:3–4), but Cain gains no such favor for his plant produce. We are not told why.

In this first mention of anger in the Bible, God addresses a resentful Cain, "If you do well, will you not be accepted?" (Gen. 4:7), and then God warns him to master the sin that is crouching at the door. But Cain gives way to jealousy and kills his brother (Gen. 4:8; cf. 1 John 3:12 and Jude 11). God responds not by demanding life for life but by intensifying the curse of toilsome work upon Cain (Gen. 4:10–12).

Adam's sin did not bring God's curse upon people, but on the ground (Gen. 3:17). Cain's sin brings the ground's curse upon Cain himself (Gen. 4:11). He can no longer be satisfied tilling the soil, so the farmer becomes a wanderer with the thistles and thorns of anger, jealousy, and the fear of retribution in him. Eventually, he settles in the land of Nod, east of Eden, where he builds the first city mentioned in the Bible (Gen. 4:16–17).

Chapter 4 then leaps forward seven generations to Cain's descendant Lamech, whose tyrannical deeds now amplify the sin of Cain. Lamech practices polygamy (Gen. 4:19), defying the purpose of marriage in Genesis 2:24 (cf. Matt. 19:5–6). And he boasts of his power to murder in retaliation for merely being struck (Gen. 4:23–24). The fruit of tree of the knowledge of good and evil proves bitter beyond anything Eve and Adam could have imagined.

 Food for Thought

What is the fruit of your work? How does God's curse on the ground compare with his curse on Cain? Why did he have spare Adam but not Cain?

_____

_____

_____

_____

_____

Idols of Aggression and Dominance

Yet in Lamech we also see the beginnings of civilization. Division of labor—which spelled trouble between Cain and Abel—leads to advances in musical instruments and metallurgy (Gen. 4:20–21). The harp and flute can be redeemed and used in the praise of God (1 Sam. 16:23), as can the metal work that went into the construction of the Hebrew tabernacle (Exod. 35:4–19, 30–35).

But Lamech's poetry in celebration of his violence points to dangers that accompany technological advance in cultures that revere the pursuit of power. Adam's hope for the redemption of his race promised by God is the last concern of the chapter, and we are pointed to the descendants of his son Seth and away from Cain (Gen. 4:25–26).

 Food for Thought

How would you characterize the culture in your workplace? Does it stratify the workers in some hierarchy of importance or celebrate the contributions of each specialized task group equally? What are the blessings or curses you experience because of that culture? What roles can Christians undertake in regard to the cultures they must work in?

Prayer

Pause for a few moments of silence to reflect on what you've just studied. Then offer a prayer, either spontaneous or by using the following:

Lord,

As we consider the endemic worship of the aggressive, the assertive, and the tough-minded self in our culture, please help us to offer ourselves as living sacrifices, trusting you for the power of your Spirit who heals the brokenhearted and rebukes the violent, even as we seek your presence in our workplaces.

Amen.

Lesson #2: God Says "Enough!" (6:1–22)

Anarchy of Spirit and Flesh

Genesis 6 introduces us to a world of anarchy that is hard to translate. It appears to involve the interference of angelic beings, producing superhuman offspring from women they take at will, but the meaning of "sons of God" and "Nephilim" remains a speculative venture at best. The general sense of the period is the rape of the whole created order where the strong prey on the weak, vandalizing the natural world and reducing it to chaos. It is so much out of control that God's response is grief and a determination to start over, except that Noah pleased him (Gen. 6:6–8).

Through Seth, the Line of Redemption for all Creation

Since the demise of Adam and Eve, God has worked through persons willing to stand against the sin that lures humanity into forming perverse cultures. Despite Adam's failure, the line of his descendants through Seth to Noah yields "a righteous man, blameless in his generation; Noah walked with God" (Gen. 6:9).

Noah is the first person in Scripture whose work is primarily redemptive. In him we see the progenitor of priests, prophets, and apostles, called to the work of reconciliation with God, and also of environmentalists, health-care workers, and all others called to the work of redeeming nature. To greater or lesser degrees, all workers since Noah are called to the holistic work of reconciliation and redemption.

 Food for Thought

How can we combat anarchy? What do reconciliation and redemption look like in your work environment?

_____

_____

_____

_____

_____

_____

_____

_____

Reconciliation and Redemption Are Costly

God calls Noah to build an ark—and what a building project it is! Against the jeers of neighbors, Noah and his sons must fell thousands of cypress trees, then hand-make them into planks enough to build a floating zoo. This three-deck vessel needs the capacity to carry all the various species of animals and to store all of the food and water required for an indefinite period. Despite the hardship, the text assures us that "Noah did this; he did all that God commanded him" (Gen. 6:13–22).

In the business world, entrepreneurs take risks with long-term goals, working beyond conventional wisdom to develop new products or processes. Here, Noah faces an apparently impossible task, and the jeers of his peers, with a faith and tenacity perhaps requiring a hundred years for completion.

 Food for Thought

How does the holistic nature of Noah's mission inform our mission as Christians in the twenty-first century? What might happen if the church saw its role as including the encouraging and the helping of innovators in business, science, academia, arts, government, and the other spheres of work?

_____

_____

_____

_____

_____

Prayer

Pause for a few moments of silence to reflect on what you've just studied. Then offer a prayer, either spontaneous or by using the following:

> *Lord,*
>
> *Daily we are made aware of national powers resorting to aggression, the misuse of astonishing technologies, resentful people resorting to terrorism, the despoiling of natural resources. Please grant us a vision for how our mission as Christians might bring redemption and reconciliation where it is most needed in our own time.*
>
> *Amen.*

Lesson #3: God Creates a New World (7:1–8:19)

A New World Foreshadowing the Ultimate Renewal of Creation

Just as Noah an   his family complete the ark, a constant deluge of rain brings mass extinction of created life and floats the ark on ever-rising waters. The inundation keeps it afloat, even above mountains, for more than half a year. For Noah and his family and the animals on board it is a safe ride through an extraordinary judgment that brings them to the beginning of a new epoch in human history.

When at last the flood subsides, the ground is dry and new vegetation is springing up. The occupants of the ark emerge to walk upon land once again. The text echoes Genesis 1, emphasizing the continuity of creation. God blows a "wind over the deep and the waters" recede (Gen. 8:1–3). Yet it is truly for them a new world, reshaped by the force of the floods. God gives humanity opportunity to begin again its growth and development of culture, this time with reverence for their Creator.

What may be less apparent is that the building of the ark, the first recorded large-scale engineering work, is an environmental project as well as an ethical and cultural one. God assigns a human being the task of saving the animals and trusts him to do it faithfully. We have not been released from God's call to "have dominion over the fish of the sea and the birds of the air and over every living thing that moves upon the earth" (Gen. 1:28). Rather, God is always at work to restore what was lost in the Fall; and in making redemption possible in Christ from the very beginning, he uses those who believe in him as his chief instruments in that restorative work.

In Noah's story, we see a foreshadowing of an ultimate perfection and healing of the material world from the effects of the Fall, *within* our cosmos, through someone greater than Noah. We get our best glimpse of this in the last book of the Bible, Revelation 21 and 22.

 Food for Thought

The story of Noah is variously told as a great tale for children and an extraordinary subject for a Hollywood blockbuster. But we see him now as a participant in judgment and agent for renewal of the creation mandate in a new world. What environmental, ethical, or cultural renewals are needed where you work? How is God's creativity working in you to help bring about these renewals?

_____

_____

_____

_____

Prayer

Pause for a few moments of silence to reflect on what you've just studied. Then offer a prayer, either spontaneous or by using the following:

> *Lord,*
>
> *You are concerned for your entire material world, a world that mankind has constantly exploited for the exclusive benefit of one group or another. Help us develop the corporate responsibility as your church to contradict and challenge everything that despoils the beauty and wonder of the world you made for us to care for.*
>
> *Amen.*

Chapter 6

God Works to Keep His Promise—Part 1

(Genesis 8–10)

Lesson #1: God's Covenant with Noah (8:20–9:17)

The Creation Mandate Continues, Only More So

When the ark comes to rest on the mountains of Ararat, more than a month passes by before Noah and those on board the ark are given the all clear by God to exit and stand on dry land. Noah immediately builds an altar to the Lord (Gen. 8:20) and offers sacrifices of some of the animals, which pleases God. In some way, this anticipates the blood sacrifice for the forgiveness of sin instituted much later by Moses with the Israelites. It's a good start from a man who is like a new Adam. There is the humility of admitting the fallen nature in himself and his family and honoring symbolically God's requirement of atonement for their sin.

Food for Thought

How do we symbolically honor God's atonement for our sin?

_____

_____

_____

_____

God resolves never again to bring such devastation to humanity or the other creatures (Gen. 8:22). Then God binds himself to a covenant with Noah and his descendants, promising never to destroy the earth by flood (Gen. 9:8–17). God gives the bow in the clouds as a sign of his promise.

Although the earth has radically changed, God's purposes for work remain the same. He repeats his blessing and promise to "Noah and his sons with him" that they will "be fruitful and multiply, and fill the earth" (Gen. 9:1, 9:7). He affirms his promise of provision of food through their work (Gen. 9:3). In return, he sets requirements for justice among people and for the protection of all creatures (Gen. 9:4–6).

It is worth noting that the Hebrew word translated as "rainbow" actually omits the sense of "rain." It refers simply to a bow—a battle and hunting tool. Bible scholar Bruce Waltke notes that in ancient Near East mythologies, stars in the shape of a bow were associated with the anger or hostility of the god, but that "here the warrior's bow is hung up, pointed away from the earth." Another scholar, Meredith Kline, observes that "the symbol of divine bellicosity and hostility has been transformed into a token of reconciliation between God and man." The relaxed bow stretches from earth to heaven, from horizon to horizon. An instrument of war becomes a symbol of peace through God's covenant with Noah.

 *Food for Thought*

Noah begins his role as a new Adam in a new world with the same creation mandate given to Adam and Eve. But his first act is priestly, acknowledging the sin affecting himself and all his family and making a sacrificial atonement. Why do you think this pleases God, and what might it suggest for Christians in the workplace?

_____

_____

_____

_____

_____

_____

Prayer

Pause for a few moments of silence to reflect on what you've just studied. Then offer a prayer, either spontaneous or by using the following:

Lord,

How easily we forget that being fruitful and multiplying is your mandate and that you long to see us honoring it wherever we are found. Please help us to do the priestly work of receiving and offering your covenantal forgiveness in Christ, wherever you place us.

Amen.

Lesson #2: Noah's Fall (9:20–29)

Greatness Can Bring Moral Vulnerability

In the new world after the flood Noah becomes a farmer. One of the innovations he brings to the new world is wine production. And his excessive drinking of it is the trigger for a major family tragedy. Becoming drunk, Noah passes out, naked, in his tent. Noah's son Ham enters the tent and finds Noah in this drunken nakedness, and at some point he alerts his brothers. The other two circumspectly enter the tent backwards and cover up their father without looking at his nakedness.

It is difficult for modern readers to make out quite why this is such an issue, but Noah and his sons clearly understand it to be a family disaster. When Noah regains consciousness he knows an evil was done to him, and his response permanently destroys the family's tranquility. Noah curses Ham's descendants via Ham's son Canaan and destines them as slaves to the family line of his other two sons, Shem and Japheth. This sets the stage for thousands of years of enmity, war, and atrocity among the descendants of Noah.

Noah may be the first person of great stature in ancient literature to crash into disgrace, but we are all too aware that this pattern persists to the present day. Greatness can make people vulnerable to moral failure, especially in personal and family life. The phenomenon is common enough to spawn proverbs, whether biblical ("Pride goes before destruction, and a haughty spirit before a fall," Prov. 16:18) or colloquial ("The bigger they come, the harder they fall").

Food for Thought

How can we avoid great moral failures?

_____

_____

_____

_____

_____

_____

People who exercise increasing power seem to become increasingly vulnerable to personal temptation. Noah literally saves the world and then succumbs to substance abuse and an episode of being naked in the wrong place and the wrong time with the wrong person. How many great leaders in business, government, entertainment, academia, and the church have fallen to the same temptations in our day? As our power grows, do we outgrow our ability to distinguish right and wrong?

Or perhaps Noah simply sank into apathy after his great task was accomplished. The transition from exhilarating seasons of high performance into mundane times can seem to blur the sense of our identity and with that our sense of boundaries. Perhaps it happened for Noah in the quiet aftermath of the cataclysmic reboot of creation—and wine was his prop. In any case, it warns us to be watchful in our own work.

The Bible offers no easy answer to such questions, and even Jesus was tempted to misuse his power (Matt. 4:1–11). The only protection seems to be to draw ever closer to God in prayer (Luke 22:39–44).

Food for Thought

When do you find yourself most likely to need reinforcement of your sense of purpose, and how do you respond when your sense of self feels weak and blurred? Is it a person, a substance, a behavior you turn to as a prop? What is your best strategy for dealing with this?

_____

_____

_____

_____

_____

_____

_____

Prayer

Pause for a few moments of silence to reflect on what you've just studied. Then offer a prayer, either spontaneous or by using the following:

Lord,

In the weariness after great trials and challenges can come a weirdly, ill-defined sense of self and longing for cheap consolations. With greatness can come a sense of doing things out of bounds simply because we think, like little gods, that we can. Please help us to stay awake, watch and pray, and know our limits, so we can maintain the grace and favor of Christ among our peers and families.

Amen.

Lesson #3: Noah's Children and the Nations from Them (Genesis 10)

Where Redemption Will Not Be Found: Empires

In what is sometimes called the "Table of Nations," Genesis 10 traces first the descendants of Japheth (Gen. 10:2–5), then the descendants of Ham (Gen. 10:6–20), and finally the descendants of Shem (Gen. 10:21–31). We are meant to notice that the line through which God's redemptive plan runs (the line of Shem) is a line that rejects the grossly violent, the flagrantly immoral, and the boldly autonomous descendants of Adam. Among them, Ham's grandson Nimrod stands out as a warning to us that must be accounted in our theology of work.

Nimrod is a tyrant who gains infamy in his own period of history, a mighty hunter to be feared, and most significantly, a builder of many cities (Gen. 10:8–12). Nimrod founds an empire of naked aggression, which he begins in the city of Babel and later expands through a chain of cities from the territory called Shinar to the region known as Assyria. In the next chapter we will see God confront the enterprise of consolidating power in this way.

 Food for Thought

How can you be an agent of change in a corrupt culture? How can we hold others accountable to protect the innocent?

_____

_____

_____

_____

_____

So what is the problem with this ambition arising from mankind as image-bearer to build cities and consolidate power in empires? The problem is that empires founded on one person's power are doomed to fail. As the examples of Al Dunlap (Sunbeam), Jeff Skilling (Enron), Frank Lorenzo (Eastern Airlines), and countless others show, when a business empire is founded on the ambition of one person, it will collapse as soon as that individual no longer has an advantage over the rest of the world. Lorenzo, for example, built an empire based on his unique willingness and ability to take over troubled airlines and cut labor costs through strikebreaking, if necessary. His strategy succeeded at Continental Airlines but failed at Eastern Airlines, where a combination of union confrontations, congressional investigations, and passenger dissatisfaction stalled his plan and led to Eastern's bankruptcy and liquidation.

General Peter Pace, former chairman of the U.S. Joint Chiefs of Staff, says that even in a hierarchical organization, good leadership does not come from strong-arming other people. As a platoon leader in Vietnam, he was enraged when an enemy sniper killed one of his men. "I called in an artillery strike to get the sniper," Pace recounts. "Then I looked to one of my sergeants. He did not say a thing, but he simply looked at me, and I knew what I was about to do was wrong. I called off the artillery strike, and we swept the village. We found nothing but women and children, as the sniper was long gone. I don't know that I could have lived with myself had I done what I originally planned to do."

Whether in business, government, the military, or any other sphere of work, exercising dominion as God intended does not come from amassing and exercising individual power. Dominion means orchestrating relationships among the many people whose gifts are needed to achieve the long-term purposes of developing natural and human potential. It is comes not from concentrating power but from dispersing responsibility wisely.

 Food for Thought

We hear a lot today about the culture of a workplace and its effects, positive or negative, upon the mission of the organization. How does the warning about Nimrod inform your appreciation for the culture of your workplace? What issues might we need to resolve for both the economic growth and well-being of the people in our organizations?

_____

_____

_____

_____

_____

Prayer

Pause for a few moments of silence to reflect on what you've just studied. Then offer a prayer, either spontaneous or by using the following:

Lord,

Make me able to recognize when the culture I work in opposes your redemption of the earth and its people. Help me to take action with others who are called like me to be agents of the city of God, yet to be revealed from heaven when Christ returns.

Amen

Chapter 7

God Works to Keep His Promise—Part 2

(Genesis 11)

Lesson #1: The Tower of Babel—the Hubris (11:1–5)

Driven by Fear and Fame

Although God does not condemn this drive to reach the heavens, the project seems misdirected.

> "Let us build ourselves a city, and a tower with its top in the heavens, and let us make a name for ourselves; otherwise we shall be scattered abroad upon the face of the whole earth."
>
> (Gen. 11:3–4)

What did they want? Fame? What did they fear? Being scattered without the security of numbers in world of wild beasts and hostile neighbors? The tower they proposed to build seemed huge to them, but the Genesis narrator wryly mentions it was so tiny that God had to "come down to see it" (Gen. 11:5). It's a very different city from the New Jerusalem of peace, order, and virtue to be unveiled at Christ's return.

Reversing the Cultural Mandate

God's objection to the tower is that it will give the people the expectation that "nothing they plan to do will be impossible for them" (Gen. 11:6). Like Adam and Eve before them, they intend to use the creative power they possess as image-bearers of God to act *against* God's purposes. It's a reversal of the cultural mandate. Instead of filling the earth, they intend to concentrate themselves in one location. Instead of exploring the fullness of the name God gave them—*adam*, "humanity" (Gen. 5:2)—they decide to make a name for themselves above the rest.

God judges their arrogance and ambition as out of bounds and does two things. He confuses their language so that understanding becomes difficult, and he scatters them abroad so that they begin to fill the earth (Gen. 11:8–9).

 Food for Thought

Fear of others and inordinate ambition have a terrible way of distorting work environments, making the fortunes of the organization more important than the service or the product for the clients. Assess your own workplace in this regard. How much does fear of competitors and desire for reputation affect the delivery service or product to your client group?

_____

_____

_____

_____

_____

_____

_____

Prayer

Pause for a few moments of silence to reflect on what you've just studied. Then offer a prayer, either spontaneous or by using the following (from Psalm 56:3–4):

Lord,

When I am afraid, I put my trust in you. In God whose word I praise, in God I put my trust; I shall not be afraid. What can mere man do to me?

Amen.

Lesson #2: The Tower of Babel—God's Visitation (11:5–9)

The Mercy of God's Judgment

In *The Brothers Karamazov*, Fyodor Dostoevsky wrote, "Without God and the future life, it means everything is permitted." Sometimes God will not give us our way because his mercy toward us is too great. God saw that if people were allowed to complete the Tower of Babel, "nothing they plan to do will be impossible for them" (Gen. 11:6). A moment's reflection on the horrors we have experienced in our own lifetime assist us to recognize the mercy in God preventing everything from becoming instantly possible for us.

It helps to recall that the people of the City of Babel were all descendants of Noah through his three sons. But after God's interference they abandoned the construction of the tower of Babel, and the three tribal groups migrated to different parts of the Middle East: Japheth's descendants moved west into Anatolia (Turkey) and Greece; Ham's descendants went south into Arabia and Egypt; and Shem's descendants remained in the east in what we know today as Iraq. From these three genealogies in Genesis 10, we discover where the tribal and national divisions of the ancient Near East developed.

Does the failure of their Babel project mean that city building is bad? Clearly no. God gave Israel their capital city of Jerusalem, and the ultimate home of God's people is God's own city coming down from heaven (Rev. 21:2). The idea of "city" is not inherently evil, but the pride that we can attach to cities displeases God (Gen. 4:12–14). Theologian Bruce Waltke concludes from the Babel story:

> Society apart from God is totally unstable. On the one hand, people earnestly seek existential meaning and security in their collective unity. On the other hand, they have an insatiable appetite to consume what others possess. . . . At the heart of the city of man is love for self and hatred for God. The city reveals that the human spirit will not stop at anything short of usurping God's throne in heaven.

 Food for Thought

Even when we see the benefits of God's limits for us, what attracts us to autonomy? What other entities are not inherently evil but associate with ideas displeasing to God?

_____

_____

_____

_____

_____

_____

Redirection Back to His Plan

As with the expulsion from Eden, God's scattering of the peoples is merciful as punishment and loaded with redemption. From the beginning, God intended people to disperse across the world. "Be fruitful and multiply, and fill the earth" (Gen. 1:28). By scattering people so that their work of hubris was abandoned, God redirected them back to his own plan, which results in the beautiful array of peoples and cultures that populate the earth today.

And so we can see in hindsight how necessary it was for the Babel project to be thwarted. The scale of evils worked by humanity in the twentieth and twenty-first centuries alone is a demonstration of what people do when they develop technologies as a substitute for acknowledging dependence on true Creator God (Gen. 11:6). Oppression and violence reign.

 Food for Thought

It is amazing that each time we see God act in judgment in Genesis 1–11 it is a mercy to the human race. At Babel, tyranny was frustrated and humanity was freed to fulfill its diverse callings again. What takeaway is there for you in the Babel story when you consider the organization where you work?

_____

_____

_____

_____

_____

Prayer

Pause for a few moments of silence to reflect on what you've just studied. Then offer a prayer, either spontaneous or by using the following:

Lord,

So often, my career ambitions are inordinate and proud. Please assist me to find my name and reputation in Christ, yoked with him in the humility of serving others.

Amen.

Lesson #3: Redemption Planned through Shem (11:10–32)

What can we learn from the failure of the tower of Babel for our work today? First, the builders disobeyed God's command to spread out and fill the earth. They centralized their geographical dwellings, their culture, language, and institutions. In their ambition to do one great thing ("make a name for ourselves"), they stifled the breadth of endeavor that ought to come with the varieties of gifts, services, activities, and functions with which God endows people (1 Cor. 12:4–11).

 Food for Thought

How can we avoid the sin of "making a name for ourselves"?

_____

_____

_____

_____

_____

_____

_____

_____

Although God wants people to work together for the common good (Gen. 2:18; 1 Cor. 12:8), he has not created us to accomplish it through the centralization and accumulation of power. He warned the people of Israel against the dangers of concentrating power in a king other than himself (1 Sam. 10–18). God has prepared for us a divine king, Christ our Lord, and under him there is no place for great concentrations of power in a leaders, institutions, or governments.

We might then expect Christian leaders and institutions to be careful to disperse authority and to favor coordination, common goals and values, and democratic decision making, instead of a concentration of power. But sadly this is not always the case. All too often, Christians have sought the same kind of concentration of power that tyrants and authoritarians seek, assuming that their more apparently benevolent goals justify their culturally bound means of getting there.

In this mode, Christian legislators seek control over the populace, like their secular counterparts, but with the object of enforcing piety or morality. In this mode, Christian businesspeople seek as much as others to corner the market, although for the apparently benevolent purpose of enhancing quality, customer service, or ethical behavior. In this mode, Christian educators seek to restrict thought as authoritarian educators do but with the plausibly good intent of enforcing moral expression, kindness, and sound doctrine. These are strange ironies.

 *Food for Thought*

Can Christians in power use their ends to justify their means? How does a biblical community—such as the church—differ from concentrated power?

_____

_____

_____

_____

_____

As praiseworthy as their goals may be, the events of the tower of Babel suggest that they are dangerously misguided. (God's later warning to Israel about the dangers of having a king echo this suggestion; see 1 Samuel 10:8–18.) Since Christians are sinful too, albeit as people made capable of overcoming sin, God's plan for human dominion prefers the dispersal of people, power, authority, and capabilities, rather than concentrating it in one person, institution, party, or movement.

Of course, some situations demand decisive exercise of power by one person or a small group. An air traffic controller would be a fool to have the pilot take a vote of the passengers to decide which runway to land on! But could it be, more often than we realize, that when we are in positions of power, God is calling us to disperse, delegate, authorize, and train others, rather than exercising all power ourselves? Doing so feels messy, inefficient, hard to measure, risky and anxiety inducing. But it seems to be in these modes of exercising our power that we discover the leading of God's spirit, the miracle of redemption and reconciliation at work in our leadership.

Food for Thought

Discuss the structure of the organization where you work. Then consider the means by which it aims to achieve its goals. Is there a concentration of power at the top of the hierarchy of power? How does that affect morale in the workplace? Or is there a wide group of decision makers representing the people who do the work? If so, how does that play out in terms of workplace productivity? Is there need for reform, and if so, how might that be encouraged?

_____

_____

_____

_____

_____

_____

Prayer

Pause for a few moments of silence to reflect on what you've just studied. Then offer a prayer, either spontaneous or by using the following:

Lord,

We are not very creative when it comes to fulfilling the cultural mandate, and we often borrow means to our gospel-inspired ends from our surrounding culture. Please show us the way to repentance and reform where power and control have become central and aggressive in our various organizations.

Amen.

Chapter 8

Conclusions from Genesis 1–11

Lesson #1: Revisiting Genesis 1–3

The Creation Mandate Reprised

In the opening chapters of the Bible, God creates the world and brings us forth to join him in further creativity. He creates us in his image to exercise dominion, to be fruitful and multiply, to receive his provision, to work in relationship with him and with other people, and to observe the limits of his creation. He equips us with resources, abilities, and communities to fulfill these tasks and gives us the pattern of working toward them six days out of seven. He gives us the freedom to do these things out of love for him and his creation, which also gives us the freedom to *not* do the things he created us for.

To our lasting injury, the first human beings chose to violate God's mandate, and since then people have continued to choose disobedience—to a greater or lesser degree. As a result, our work has become less productive, more toilsome, and less satisfying, and our relationships and work are diminished and at times even destructive.

 Food for Thought

Consider what it means to be made in the image of God in its five dimensions, which are repeated in each of the two presentations of the creation in Genesis 1–2. What metaphors can you think of to explain the height of that original estate of Adam and Eve? Now consider what might be different in the outworking of your own field of work had they remained faithful to the mandate given them. Describe what it might be like. (Two books that can assist our imaginations in entering the pristine world of Eden are C. S. Lewis's *Perelandra: The Voyage to Venus* and chapters 8–9 of *The Magician's Nephew* of his Narnia Chronicles, and the biblical book "Song of Songs" also portrays a man and a woman working together in a nearly ideal situation.)

_____

_____

_____

_____

_____

_____

_____

Prayer

Lord Jesus Christ,

It is when we look at you that we see what we might have been had our first parents obeyed you from the beginning. Thank you for coming to rescue us and empowering us through your Spirit to endure the frustration of all that is broken and in need of constant repair. Thank you for the hope of ultimately working from your city of righteousness where all works together for human flourishing.

Amen.

Lesson #2: God's Response to the Fall in Genesis 3

Redemption Begins

Despite the catastrophic decision of Adam and Eve to separate themselves from the very source of their lives, we see in the spare text of Genesis 3 and into 4 that God continues to call Adam, Eve, and their descendants to work, to equip them, and to provide for their needs.

Many of us, especially in the West, experience this reality in the opportunity to do good, creative, fulfilling work that provides for their needs and contributes to a thriving community. Yet throughout the world many more suffer dire poverty because of misrule, oppression, discrimination, and other abuses by people in power that subvert God's gift of work and impede the cultural mandate.

 Food for Thought

How can we contribute to global efforts to fulfill the creation mandate?

_____

_____

_____

_____

_____

_____

The New Necessity of Our Work

Therefore, the Fall has made the work that began in the Garden of Eden more necessary than ever. Work has become toil because we work against God's purposes and violate the relationships inherent in work. Because of the Fall, we find ourselves at work in a partially hostile natural world, constrained by corrupt social systems in business government, finance, education, politics, health, agriculture, law, environmental care, and every other field of human endeavor. One of our tasks now is to understand the effects of the Fall in enough detail to participate in God's practical work of putting the creation back on track.

Although Christians have sometimes misunderstood this, God did not respond to the Fall by withdrawing from the material world and confining his interests to some disembodied spiritual realm. As we see in Genesis, God who is Spirit immerses himself in creating from formless matter the forms of life that make for us a world, and who remains at work in the world after humanity's disobedience. Later in the Bible, we see in Jesus this same Creator entering the material world and ennobling it and our human form by his life and work as a human being.

Work, including the relationships that enrich it and the limits that bless it, remains God's gift to us, even if it is severely marred by the conditions of existence after the Fall. It is noteworthy that this same Jesus commissioned his followers to work in groups, loving one another as they set out to make disciples of the nations (Luke 10:1–17). It must surely be a part of our Christian mission to work corporately and lovingly to extend the opportunity of work, including repair work, to the next generations.

Food for Thought

Recall your perspective on work before you began this study. Has it changed? What have you learned that is newly informing your attitude to your work? How do you think it will affect what you continue to do as work?

_____

_____

_____

_____

_____

_____

_____

Prayer

Pause for a few moments of silence to reflect on what you've just studied. Then offer a prayer, either spontaneous or by using the following:

Lord Jesus Christ,

Your willingness to immerse yourself in the broken life of Palestine two thousand years ago informs us in our own time. You have gifted us so differently that you must have so many diverse calls for people of every tribe and tongue in fulfilling the Creation mandate. Please help us see how the gospel brings with it both creation and repair work, and lead us into it.

Amen.

Lesson #3: From a New Start in Noah to the Babel Debacle (Gen. 4–11)

Sovereign and Attentive to Every Detail

These eight chapters of Genesis show us how actively God remains at work to redeem his creation from the effects of the Fall—how attentively he watches over work, and how decisively he exercises his power to order and reorder the world and its inhabitants.

In the flood and Babel stories, we see God's sovereignty over the created world and over every living creature, spirit, human and otherwise. God's primary focus is tending to his own image in humanity and the outworking of the destiny of those who acknowledge him in faithfulness to their created purpose.

 Food for Thought

What does it look like to acknowledge God in faithfulness to your creative purpose?

_____

_____

_____

_____

_____

_____

_____

Judgment Promoting Redemption

Mercifully, God does not tolerate human efforts to "be like God" (Gen. 3:4). God's judgment is against every human effort to acquire excessive power and substitute self-sufficiency for relationship with him. This is a warning to every generation.

Our aim, like Noah's, is to receive work as a gift from God and humble ourselves so as to work according to his direction and seek blessing and fruitfulness in our work. Biblical history suggests that this fruitfulness may not be realized in our lifetimes—it may be awaiting its unveiling in future generations or when the kingdom of God is fully come. Therefore, by God's help, we pray to be unlike the builders of the Tower of Babel—those who tried to grasp renown, power, and success on their own terms, bringing violence and frustration upon themselves and others.

Like all the characters in these chapters of Genesis, we face the choice of whether to work with God or in opposition to him. Working with God means to work according to God's purposes *in* the world, *on* the world, *with* the world, and *for* the world.

Genesis, by its name, is the beginning of the story. How the story of God's work to redeem his creation ultimately turns out is told through the remaining sixty-five books of the Bible. From them we know that it leads to the restoration of the created world—including the work of God's creatures—as God has intended from the beginning.

 ### Food for Thought

Perhaps this study of Genesis 1–11 has raised questions for you in regard to the ministry of Jesus as he carried on the work of redeeming the creation. What new insights, thoughts, or questions do you have concerning work and its role in Jesus' Great Commission to "make disciples of all nations" and to "teach them to obey everything I have commanded you" (Matt. 28:19–20)? How will you implement the insights or what steps might you take to develop these thoughts? And how might your questions be answered?

_____

_____

_____

_____

_____

_____

_____

Prayer

Pause for a few moments of silence to reflect on what you've just studied. Then offer a prayer, either spontaneous or by using the following:

Lord,

We acknowledge that familiarity with the Bible is often an obstacle to our understanding. From this Genesis story we now stop to acknowledge the extraordinary care you have for us. You put us here as co-laborers in your world's growth and development until its purpose is made complete. Grant us to take from here new understandings, so that we truly do make a difference in the places you have called us to work.

Amen.

Wisdom for Using This Study in the Workplace

Community within the workplace is a good thing and a Christian community within the workplace is even better. Sensitivity is needed, however, when we get together in the workplace (even a Christian workplace) to enjoy fellowship time together, learn what the Bible has to say about our work, and encourage one another in Jesus' name. When you meet at your place of employment, here are some guidelines to keep in mind:

- *Be sensitive to your surroundings.* Know your company policy about having such a group on company property. Make sure not to give the impression that this is a secret or exclusive group.

- *Be sensitive to time constraints.* Don't go over your allotted time. Don't be late to work! Make sure you are a good witness to the others (especially non-Christians) in your workplace by being fully committed to your work during working hours and doing all your work with excellence.

- *Be sensitive to the shy or silent members of your group.* Encourage everyone in the group and give them a chance to talk.

- *Be sensitive to the others by being prepared.* Read the Bible study material and Scripture passages and think about your answers to the questions ahead of time.

These Bible studies are based on the *Theology of Work Bible Commentary*. Besides reading the commentary, please visit the Theology of Work website (www.theologyofwork.org) for videos, interviews, and other material on the Bible and your work.

Leader's Guide

Living Word. It is always exciting to start a new group and study. The possibilities of growth and relationship are limitless when we engage with one another and with God's word. Always remember that God's word is "living and active, sharper than any two-edged sword" (Heb. 4:12). When you study his word, it should change you.

A Way Has Been Made. Please know that you and each person joining your study have been prayed for by people you will probably never meet but who share your faith. And remember that it is "the LORD who goes before you. He will be with you; he will not fail you or forsake you. Do not fear or be dismayed" (Deut. 31:8). As a leader, you need to know that truth. Remind yourself of it throughout this study.

Pray. It is always a good idea to pray for your study and those involved weeks before you even begin. It is recommended that you pray for yourself as leader, your group members, and the time you are about to spend together. It's no small thing you are about to start and the more you prepare in the Spirit, the better. Apart from Jesus, we can do nothing. Remain in him and you will "bear much fruit" (John 15:5). It's also a good idea to have trusted friends pray and intercede for you and your group as you work through the study.

Spiritual Battle. Like it or not, the Bible teaches that we are in the middle of a spiritual battle. The enemy would like nothing more than for this study to be ineffective. It would be part of his scheme to have group members not show up or engage in any discussion. His victory would be that your group passes time together going through the motions of just another Bible study. You, as a leader, are a threat to the enemy as it is your desire to lead people down the path of righteousness (as taught in Proverbs). Read Ephesians 6:10–20 and put your armor on.

Scripture. Prepare before your study by reading the selected Scripture verses ahead of time.

Chapters. Each chapter contains three lessons. As you work through the lessons, keep in mind the particular chapter theme in connection with the lessons. These lessons are designed so that you can go through them in thirty minutes each.

Lessons. Each lesson has teaching points with their own discussion questions. This format should keep the participants engaged with the text and one another.

Food for Thought. The questions at the end of the teaching points are there to create discussion and deepen the connection between each person and the content being addressed. You know the people in your group and should feel free to come up with your own questions or adapt the ones provided to best meet the needs of your group. Again, this would require some preparation beforehand.

Opening and Closing Prayers. Sometimes prayer prompts are given before and usually after each lesson. These are just suggestions. You know your group and the needs present, so please feel free to pray accordingly.

Bible Commentary. The Theology of Work series contains a variety of books to help you apply the Scriptures and Christian faith to your work. This Bible study is based on the *Theology of Work Bible Commentary*, which examines what the Bible says about work. This commentary is intended to assist those with theological training or interest to conduct in-depth research into passages or books of Scripture.

Video Clips. The Theology of Work website (www.theologyofwork.com) provides good video footage of people from the marketplace highlighting teaching on work from every book of the Bible. It would be great to incorporate some of these videos into your teaching time.

Enjoy Your Study! Remember that God's word does not return void—ever. It produces fruit and succeeds in whatever way God has intended it to succeed.

> "So shall my word be that goes out from my mouth;
>   it shall not return to me empty,
>   but it shall accomplish that which I purpose,
>   and shall succeed in the thing for which I sent it." (Isa. 55:11)

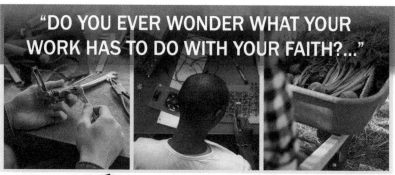